Love in Christianity and Islam

Love
in
Christianity
and
Islam

A contribution to religious ethics

by Mahnaz Heydarpoor

New City

London   Dublin

First published in Great Britain by
New City
57 Twyford Avenue
London W3 9PZ

Cover picture by Rumold van Geffen
Cover design by Tomeu Mayans

A catalogue reference for this book is available
from the British Library.

ISBN 0 904287 79 3

Typeset in Great Britain by New City

Printed and bound in Great Britain by
The Cromwell Press, Trowbridge, Wiltshire

Contents

Dedication

In the name of God, the most Beneficent,
the most Merciful

This book is dedicated
to the blessed memory of two of the greatest teachers
and examples of ethical values throughout
the history of mankind:
Jesus
and
Muhammad.

May God's Mercy and Peace be upon them
and those who truthfully follow them!

Preface

The subject covered by this book is of great importance. It seeks to show how love is at the heart of the spirituality and ethics of two great faiths, between which greater mutual understanding is urgently needed.

Relations between Christians and Muslims have suffered the effects of an historical legacy of suspicion and hatred arising from times when the great empires and civilisations associated with each found themselves in confrontation and conflict. The Muslim conquest of the Iberian peninsula, the Crusades, the fall of Constantinople, the ambitions of the Ottoman Empire and of 19th and 20th century Western imperialism, have all left a residue of bitterness and hostility. This continues to manifest itself today in the Middle East, in the Balkans and in various other parts of the world. In western societies the media's reporting of the violent activities of extremist Islamists has tended, quite unjustly, to associate Islam and Muslims with a fanaticism that is far removed from love. It is as if the relations between Catholics and Protestants in Northern Ireland were to typify Christianity.

Despite these unfortunate features, there are other much more positive aspects of the history of relations between the two faiths and their civilisations. It is all too easy to forget the many forms of mutual intellectual and cultural enrichment they have shared in art, architecture, philosophy, mathematics, science and literature over the centuries.

The areas of theological agreement between them (and also with Judaism), have also been too little appreciated. They have a common acceptance of biblical revelation and the prophetic tradition; a joint affirmation of belief in the God of Abraham; and a strong emphasis on the importance of honouring God in worship and leading a way of life directed by his law. The similarity and indeed interaction of the thought and spirituality of some of their greatest teachers and mystics during the medieval period seems also to have been quietly forgotten.

However, in the changing ethos of the more religiously pluralistic, post-colonial situation in the West and the greater sense of global community brought about by better communications, attitudes are rapidly changing. Dialogue between faiths and a will to seek true understanding, freed from ancient and modern stereotypes, has come much more to the fore in the West, thanks to the work of such scholars as John Esposito and Ninian Smart. Although the growth of Islamic communities in European societies has not been without its problems and tensions, a strong will is emerging among the younger generations to forge a future together based upon mutual respect for and learning from, each others' faiths and cultures.

It is in this spirit that this book is written. In view of the serious problems that have arisen between Iran, the U.S.A. and the U.K. over the past two decades, it is all the more significant that it is the work of a young Iranian Shi'ite scholar, Mahnaz Heydarpoor. A graduate of the famous University of Qum, who came to Britain with her husband and family in 1997, she soon displayed an interest in undertaking further study and research. It has been a great pleasure for me to act as her supervisor and to meet both Mahnaz and her husband Mohammad

Shomali, himself a respected scholar. They have both been excellent ambassadors for Iran and for Islam and I have learned more from them about the character and spirit of Islam than from reading many books.

Mahnaz's eager determination to deepen her understanding of Christianity and the vigour and energy with which she has pursued this aim, not only by consulting books, but by meeting Christians of differing denominational backgrounds and groups such as the Focolare Movement, has been very impressive. Her analysis of love in Christianity is scholarly and insightful, but it will be her exposition of the centrality of love in Islamic theology and ethics that will be of particular interest to many Western readers, Christians and others.

It is to be hoped that Mahnaz's initiative will be reciprocated by many more scholars searching, like her, for grounds for dialogue to further mutual appreciation and understanding between Islam and Christianity. It is also to be hoped that her warmth and generosity of spirit (in a word, her love) will also be reciprocated, so that the healing of the sad wounds inflicted by centuries of hatred and misunderstanding can be hastened for the benefit of millions.

Dr Dennis Bates,
Manchester Metropolitan University

Introduction

Every heart that is not aflame is no heart;
A frozen heart is nothing but a handful of clay.
O God! Give me a breast that sets ablaze,
And in that breast a heart, and that heart consumed with fire.
(Vahshi Kermani, 1583)

Although it might seem obvious to many people that there can be no morality without having faith or belief in God, there has always been a dispute on this subject or more generally on the relation between ethics and religion.

Among both Christian and Muslim theologians, there have been some scholars who believed in the complete dependence of morality upon divine commands and revelation, just as there have been others who believed in the autonomy of morality. According to the former, 'morally right' means 'commanded by God', and 'morally wrong' means 'forbidden by God'.

The opposite view holds that there are independent criteria of good and bad that can be understood by our reason. Accordingly, there is a possibility of having morality independent of religion. However, these people usually hold that religion can offer a clearer and more comprehensive account of morality. Both groups agree that religion provides morality with sanctions. Therefore, the debate among religious scholars is not whether religion contributes to morality or whether there is such a thing as 'religious ethics'; it is rather on the extent of this contribution.

In this book, I will try to explain the notion of religious ethics and some of its characteristics and then I will focus on the concept of love as the central concept in religious ethics. There is a shared commitment to love among all great religions of the world and this virtue of love is universally recognised. However, it is sometimes understood in different ways within different traditions. In chapters two and three, I will try to study the significance and the doctrinal foundations of love in the two great world religions: Christianity and Islam. In each case, I will study different aspects of Divine love (for Himself, for all beings and for mankind) and human love (for God and for fellow humans).

I have to say here that what I really have to do is to examine Christianity and Islam a *posteriori*, that is, in their historical development, because what we are really concerned with here is to see, for example, the actual contribution of these religions to morality. What we have to do is to make sure that we have a reliable understanding of each religion as it exists today.

To understand Christian and Islamic ethics, my research will involve some scriptural exegesis. I have relied greatly on the Bible and the Qur'an, along with *hadiths*, (narrations) as the primary sources of Christian and Islamic ethics, especially when I discuss the role of love in both religions. What I have done in this work has been to discover a generally accepted picture of love in these two religions. Unless otherwise mentioned, I have tried to refer to common points and what is acceptable to all Christians or Muslims. Indeed, in principle, there seems to be not much difference between different scholars of each religion on the subject at issue.

I realise that there has already been much research on different aspects of the topic, especially about love in

Christianity. However, I think that there is still need to undertake research like the one proposed here. One advantage of this research is that it studies the issue comparatively and not just in a single religion. The second advantage is that this research includes a discussion about the role of love in Islamic ethics, which may be unfamiliar to English-speaking readers. The third advantage is that this research enjoys access to original Islamic sources in Arabic and Persian. Thus, I hope this study can make a useful contribution to the field.

Here, I would like to mention that the question of love has been my main concern throughout my adult life. I was just 16 when I was so overwhelmed by my love for knowing God and getting close to Him that I felt I would no longer be able to continue my ordinary life. Despite all the plans that my parents and I had previously made for me, I decided to start a completely new life. With the blessing of my parents, I left my city and moved to the city of Qum, in which one of the main Islamic seminaries has existed for more than a thousand years. I devoted my life to deepening my knowledge of Islam and, more importantly, to drawing closer to God. Although I am not happy with the success that I have made, I am quite confident that I have made the best decision for myself and I have chosen the brightest way, the path of love.

During the period of research for this work, I not only read about my topic, i.e. love, but also I tried to live my topic and to witness it in the lives of others. At that time (July 1999), I spent a whole week with some Christian friends at *Mariapolis* in Windermere. There I noticed many similarities between Islam and Christianity and how a sincere love for God and fellow humans can give a new spirit to life and a new life to modern society. I was reminded of my own experience when I entered the Seminary of Qum. Now I had found others who believed in and followed the same way, the path of love.

Since then I have done my best to develop my understanding of Christianity, as it started, and as it is practised today. Not only did I make many personal friends, but also I visited various Christian organisations and places of worship and education. For example, in October 1999, I was invited to a conference on Islam and Christianity organised by the Focolare Movement in Rome. Besides the conference, I had the chance to become more familiar with the Vatican and the Roman Catholic Church. I also spent a few days in Loppiano, a small town near Florence. All the inhabitants of this town try to practise the Focolare spirituality and particularly to love God and their neighbour. Altogether I spent ten days in Italy where I also had the chance to meet Chiara Lubich, the founder of the Movement, and some of her early companions who spoke about prayer and love.

In February 2000, I spent two days at St John's College in the University of Durham, an important centre in the Church of England for the training of clergy. There I met and talked with the Rt. Revd. Stephen Sykes, the principal of St John's College and also chairman of the Doctrine Commission of the Church of England, and with Dr Croft, Dr Wakefield and a group of students.

In May 2000, I spent a whole week at Ampleforth Abbey where I had meetings with the Abbot and some of the other monks. During these meetings, I came to know more about Christian spirituality and the nature of monastic life. I must give special mention to Cyprian Smith, the author of *The Way of Paradox: Spiritual Life as Taught by Meister Eckhart* and *The Path of Life*, who kindly talked to me about Christian mysticism and the spirituality of the Benedictine order. I also benefited from the valuable books of the monastery library. In July 2000 I spent another week in *Mariapolis*, with hundreds of Catholic and Anglican Christian friends from Britain and other parts of the world in Stirling, Scotland.

I have discussed love in Christianity with many Christian friends, such as Dom Jonathan Cotton OSB, Leyland, Canon Simon Hoare, Skipton, Dimitrij Bregant, Rome, and Dom Wulstan Peterburs OSB, Ampleforth. The last three also read a draft of the chapter 'Love in Christianity' and made valuable comments. Thus, I hope I have been able to develop a fair understanding of love in Christianity as it is in theory and as it is practised today.

Finally, I would like to say that the present work was originally conceived as an M.A. dissertation (*Religious Ethics: The Contribution of Religion to Morality in Christian and Islamic Theology with Particular Reference to the Concept of Love*) and presented to the Department of Humanities and Applied Social Studies of the Manchester Metropolitan University in September 2000. In this edition, for the interest of general readers, two chapters on the classical theological views on the relation between religion and morality have been omitted.

During the period of my research, I have been helped by many people. My thanks are due to Dr Dennis Bates, who has not been just a good and benevolent supervisor and course leader, but also a friend. From the early stages of my study right up to the end he has always been available, prepared to discuss and read every bit of my work and always encouraging. My thanks are also due to the Rt. Revd. Stephen Sykes and Dr Croft for their hospitality and help during my stay at St John's College, Durham. I wish to express my thanks to the Abbot and monks of Ampleforth Abbey, especially Cyprian Smith and Wulstan Peterburs, for their hospitality and helpful discussions.

I would like also to thank all who read and made comments on the whole or part of my thesis, such as my husband Dr Mohammad A. Shomali, Canon Simon Hoare and Christina Hoare of Skipton, Dimitrij Bregant, Rome, Wulstan Peterburs OSB, Ampleforth. I am also indebted to the Imam Khomeini Education and Research Institute, Qum, Iran, for sponsoring my husband's study and our living costs, without which I would not have been able to stay here to study. I am also grateful to my husband and two sons for their love and support. I should also thank my Focolare friends, especially Frank Johnson for his sincerity and for his efforts in preparing this book for publication. And last but not least, I would extend my feelings of deep gratitude to God in place of His every favour upon us and upon all His servants, past and still remaining.

London, March 2001

Part 1

Religious Ethics

I

What does morality mean?

Before any discussion about 'religious ethics', one has
to clarify what one means by 'ethics' or 'ethical' on the
one hand and 'religion' or 'religious' on the other. In this
work I do not distinguish between 'ethical' and 'moral',
though I realise that originally these two terms came
from different roots.[1]

Morality shows people how to eradicate bad attributes
in themselves and how to foster good ones. Of course,
different moral systems may vary in their emphasis. For
example, in Western morality the greater emphasis (or
the sole emphasis) has usually been put on human
behaviour and practices. And so Paul Foulquie defines
ethics as a code of practice, the observance of which
leads human beings to their goals.[2] On the other hand,
we see that some moral systems take human characters
more seriously. For example, Sadr al-Din al-Shirazi, a
prominent Muslim philosopher, refers to human characters,
and practices originated from those characters, as two
separate subject matters of morality.[3]

To explain what type of ethical investigation is
involved here when discussing religious ethics, I have to

1 'Ethical' was derived from a Greek word for personal character, but
'moral' was derived from a Latin word for social custom. See Williams,
1997, p. 546
2 As described in Modarresi, 1997 p. 18
3 See al-Shirazi, 1378 A.H., Vol. 4, p. 116

point out that there are three types of ethical investigation: the descriptive, the normative and the meta-ethical.

Descriptive ethics is an empirical study of moral codes or practices of a certain individual or group or society or religion or the like. For example, a descriptive ethicist may undertake to provide us with an account of the morality of Socrates or Ancient Greek ethics or Islamic or even Marxist ethics. The method here is just descriptive, in order to provide an exact report on what the moral code, system or practice actually is, and not what should be there. Thus, there is no evaluative judgement required here.

Normative ethics studies moral theories on rightness and wrongness. It replies to questions such as: What makes an action morally right or wrong? Is an action good or right, if it brings about pleasure or happiness, or rather, is an action good if it is good in itself regardless of its consequences? Normative ethics also discusses the moral status of particular subjects e.g. 'Is abortion good or bad?'

Meta-ethics or analytic ethics does not deal with empirical or historical facts. Neither does it deal with any evaluative or normative judgement. It rather investigates questions about ethics such as: What is the meaning or usage of expressions such as 'right' or 'wrong'? Can moral and evaluative judgement be proved? If yes, how? What is the nature of morality? What distinguishes the moral from the non-moral? What does 'free' or 'responsible' agent mean?

Historically, moral philosophy (ethics or the philosophical study of morality) included both normative ethics and meta-ethics. However, many recent philosophers, mainly advocates of analytic philosophy, have made it exclusive to meta-ethics. They believe that philosophical study is only possible in respect of issues of meta-ethics.

Here, it is noteworthy that moral philosophers usually take a moral sentence to be a sentence which has one of the seven concepts, mentioned below, as its predicate. Those seven concepts are: good versus bad, right versus wrong, ought versus ought not, and duty. For example, 'Telling the truth is good' is a moral sentence, because its predicate is one of the moral concepts. However, 'Good is what brings about the greatest happiness for the greatest number of people' is not a moral sentence, though it is related to morality. In other words, it is meta-ethical rather than ethical.[4]

---

4 See Frankena, 1973, pp. 10 & 98

II

What does religion mean?

Having defined what is meant by 'ethics', I will now define what I mean by 'religion' or 'religious'. There are different views regarding the definition of religion, therefore a wide range of schools of thought are alleged to be 'religions'. For example, David Edwards defines religion as 'an attitude of awe towards God, or gods or the supernatural, or the mystery of life, accompanied by beliefs and affecting basic patterns of individual and group behaviour'.[5] I personally may not agree with definitions as general as this; however, I think in practice there is no need to bother ourselves about issues of general concern. I am dealing here with religion in a specific context.

Accordingly, in this work I mean by 'religion' only monotheistic religions, including Christianity and Islam; and, by 'religious ethics', I mean moral principles, codes or systems of these religions. My study of these ethical systems will be mostly descriptive, since I will explain the standpoints of Islam or Christianity or the standpoint of individual Muslims or Christians on subjects such as love.

---

5 Edwards, 1999, p. 745

III

Characteristics
of religious ethics

It has been suggested (Markham, 1998) that there are some points common to all religious moralities. Here I will explain four of them as characteristics of religious ethics: belief in a supernatural being; dependence on religious sources; believe in objectivity; and the truth value of morals, and shared concerns.

In the monotheistic religions, there is a supernatural being who has authority over human beings to tell them the sacred ideal of life and to show them the ways to reach that ideal. Followers of any religion who have some reason to believe in the truth of that religion will have no question about the authority of that source.

Religious ethics can be defined as a type of ethics that gets its validity from the religious authority. Therefore, the 'revealed' teachings of that authority have the central role in deciding what is 'right' or 'wrong'. Teachings of that authority are to be found in the scriptures of that religion such as the Bible for Christians and the Qur'an for Muslims. Of course, religious sources for ethics are not limited to the scriptures. It has been suggested (Markham, 1998) that there may be four other sources that different religious traditions use when making ethical judgements.

The second source of moral guidance is the institutions and traditions of each religion. Often these are considered as secondary (or supplementary) to the first source, i.e. the scriptures. In Christianity, for example, those in the Roman Catholic tradition talk about the Church as the mechanism provided by God to interpret the scriptures for each new age. As we will see later, in Islam, the *Sunnah* is extremely important in the formation of Islamic law.

The third source of moral guidance is human reason. The role of reason in moral guidance has to be discussed independently. However, in brief, I can say that both Judaism and Islam have an optimistic view of humanity. In both cases, the gift of human reason, which distinguishes us from the animals, is a God-given resource that should assist us in arriving at the right moral judgement. In Christianity, the issue is more complicated with the doctrine of original sin. However, the major Christian traditions share a sense that, although sin has deformed the capacity of humans to use their reason properly, it is still active. Indeed, it is this idea that leads to the Roman Catholic doctrine of natural law. The theory of natural law holds that all people everywhere, without the explicit aid of revelation, are able to partially understand moral truth. For this reason all people are without excuse. Regarding the natural moral law, the authorised view of the Roman Catholic Church is as follows:

'Man participates in the wisdom and goodness of the Creator who gives him mastery over his acts and the ability to govern himself with a view to the true and the good. The natural law expresses the original moral sense which enables man to discern by reason the good and the evil, the truth and the lie.'[6]

6 *Catechism of the Catholic Church*, 1999, no. 1954

The fourth source of moral knowledge is claimed to be the natural order. Ian Markham (1998) suggests that Roman Catholicism is the best-known tradition that uses the natural world order. He makes reference to the work of St Thomas Aquinas (following Aristotle) who believed that 'God had built into the structures of his creation the natural law' whereby 'the telos of each activity is the proper purpose for that activity.' Markham gives the well-known example of the penis, which, according to the Roman Catholic doctrine, has the telos of procreation. It is, therefore, unnatural – and thus immoral – to use the penis for other activities such as masturbation or homosexuality, or to stop the penis from carrying out its natural purpose through the use of contraception.[7]

The fifth and final source of moral values is religious experience. Some traditions believe that you can discover what God wants for you through religious experience and prayer, which can sometimes be against the accepted ethics of an age.

All the major religious traditions believe that ethical decisions are matters of truth and discovery. Although there might be some disagreements between the religions about the content of morality, there is agreement on the character of morality. They take morality to be rooted in the structure of the universe and beyond human decisions. They believe that moral values transcend human communities, grounded, in some sense, within the structures of the universe, and binding on all people everywhere.

Despite the complexity of each religion, one of the common points between all religions is that they all consider certain themes very important for all human

7 See Markham, 1998, pp. 801- 802

beings. We shall now refer to four such themes: commitment to love, the centrality of the family, the centrality of ritual, and protection of human life.

There is a shared commitment to love and compassion. Although these qualities are understood in different ways within different traditions, they are universally recognised virtues. In the next two parts of this book I will study Christian and Islamic views on love.

The second theme that is found across the major religious traditions is the centrality of the family and the complementary role of men and women. In Judaism, Christianity and Islam, Eve (representative woman) was created to help Adam (representative man). All these religions, whether they permit it or not, consider divorce undesirable.

In all these religions, ritual has a central role in forming the virtuous person. Ritual is the mechanism by which life becomes religious. Ritual relates to all aspects of life, including the start and end of life. Religious calendars involve certain rituals for days, weeks, months, and years. Fasting on certain holy days is common to most religious traditions. Rituals help in supporting morality and provide the disciplines that protect the person from evil.

Most religious traditions stress the centrality and importance of the human person and human life. Human life is considered very precious and is to be respected. This is not to say that under no conditions may human life be taken; most religious traditions allow war and capital punishment in certain circumstances. But human life is given a special status in their ethical views.

Having discussed what are usually taken as characteristics of all religious moralities, I will now elaborate more on Christian and Islamic ethics, their sources and some of the methodological questions concerning their discovery.

IV

Christian ethics

The root of Christian ethics is in the Jewish Torah, but the distinctive features of Christian ethics can best be explored by studying the teachings of Jesus in the four canonical Gospels.[8] Of course, it should be noted that there is no detailed account of the ethical teachings of Jesus in the Gospels. Preston says: "The fourth Gospel reflects in its own way the distinctive features of Jesus' ethical teaching. There is no ruling on any specific issue. The concentration is on the radical challenge Jesus brings to accepted ways [that is, Jewish ethical teaching derived from the Torah]."[9] The Sermon on the Mount (Mt. 5-7) is the most considerable collection of Jesus' teachings. Although there have been many historical and critical examinations of the Gospels, undoubtedly the most important source for Christianity today is the Bible.

To be able to study Christian ethics, besides the study of its foundation in the ministry of Jesus we have to study the interpretative parts of the New Testament. The interpreter of Jesus of whom we have most evidence is St Paul. He seems to be the first Christian who was asked to bring his understanding of the Christian ethic to bear on particular problems put forward by the churches.

---

8 Of course, there are differences between those four Gospels. As Preston puts it, the Gospel of John "can be regarded as a selective and mature series of meditations on the main themes of the first three,

V

Islamic ethics

There are two major sources for Islamic ethics: the Qur'an and the *Sunnah*. The Qur'an is regarded by Muslims as a Heavenly book, built up from and only from Divine revelation. Both the meanings and the words of the Qur'an are believed by Muslims to be from God. In practice, there is not much controversy among Muslims about the interpretation of those verses of the Qur'an that are related to morality or about the Qur'anic moral system.

The *Sunnah* can be regarded as the application of the Qur'anic teachings to the problems of life as exemplified in the Prophet's deeds, sayings and approvals (of the deeds or sayings of others in his presence). Usually, the *Sunnah* contains more details.

Among the Shi'a, the *Sunnah* includes both the *Sunnah* of the Prophet Muhammad, and his household, *ahlul-bayt*, who are considered as heirs of his knowledge and followers of his task by presenting and explaining pure Islamic teachings exactly in the way that they were revealed to him. The rich literature from Shi'a Imams on ethical issues is a great help to them in clarifying Islamic views on detailed ethical issues.

---

whether the author knew them or only the oral traditions behind them.",
Preston, 1996, p. 94

9 Preston 1996, p. 97

For the Shi'a and some other Muslims, another important source of understanding Islam is the reason or the intellect, *al-'aql*. Although the main source to emphasise on the role of reason is the Qur'an itself, there has been a dispute among Sunni theological schools of thought as to the role of reason and how to make a balance between reason and revelation. The dispute between the Ash'arites and the Mu'tazilites on this issue is quite well-known. The Shi'a have had a very clear standpoint regarding reason. There is a famous sentence among Shi'a scholars, which is quite often invoked as a rule and that is: *Kullama hakama bihi al-'aql hakama bihi al-Shar' wa kullama hakama bihi al-Shar' hakam bihi al-'aql*. It means that whatever judgement is made by reason the same is made by the religious law or *Shari'ah* and vice versa. Therefore, the approval of reason in respect of a practical issue can be taken as a proof of its permissibility in *Shari'ah*. For example, if justice is rationally good or right it would be so legally as well.

Part 2

Love in Christian Ethics

I

Pillars of Christian ethics

Christian ethics, like any other ethical system, is built around one or more virtues. In the case of Christianity, virtues have been conventionally numbered as seven, on the assumption that these seven, when combined with their opposite vices, i.e. the seven deadly sins, can explain the whole range of human conduct. The seven consist of the four 'natural' virtues, which were familiar to the old pagan world, and the three 'theological' virtues, which were specifically prescribed in Christianity. The natural virtues can be acquired through human efforts, but the theological ones arise as special gifts from God. [10]

The natural virtues are prudence, temperance, courage, and justice. This list is said to go back to Socrates and is certainly to be found in Plato and Aristotle. Christian moralists like Augustine and Thomas Aquinas found the list reasonable. To these four, Christianity added the three theological virtues of faith, hope, and love.[11] These three were originally introduced by the Apostle Paul, who not only distinguished these three as

10 According to Christian teaching, the theological virtues do not originate from natural man. They are imparted by God through Christ and are then practised by the believer. See *Britannica* 1997.

11 It has to be noted that St Thomas in the *Summa Theologica* adds to the list of virtues three intellectual virtues: wisdom, knowledge and intuition. See also Brett, 1992, p. 9

specifically Christian virtues, but singled out love as the chief of the three: 'So faith, hope, love abide, these three; but the greatest of these is love.' (1 Cor. 13: 13)

Thus, in Christianity love becomes the ruling standard, and when there is a conflict of duties, the priority must be given to love.[12] Love is so important that the whole spiritual or mystical journey is seen as one of love. Summarising what he has said in his book about mysticism, William Johnston writes:

> 'It [mysticism] is the answer to a call of love; and every stage is enlightened and guided by a living flame, a blind stirring, a love which has no reservation or restriction. This is the love which, Paul says, is superior to any charismatic gift and has no limitations whatsoever. It "bears all things, it believes all things, hopes all things, endures all things... love never ends" (I Cor. 13: 7,8).'[13]

---

12 Vincent MacNamara (1989, p. 62) holds that there has been a change in Catholic moral theology on the status of love. He believes that love has not always had this unique position in the past; there was a time when love (or charity) was considered as just one of many moral requirements.

13 Johnston, 1978, p. 135

II

Love as the basis for Christian ethics

Matthew reports Jesus as having said, in the Sermon on the Mount, that he came not to destroy the law and the prophets but to fulfil them:

> 'Think not that I have come to abolish the law and the prophets; I have come not to abolish them but to fulfil them. For truly, I say to you, till heaven and earth pass away, not an iota, not a dot, will pass from the law until all is accomplished. Whoever then relaxes one of the least of these commandments and teaches men so, shall be called least in the kingdom of heaven; but he who does them and teaches them shall be called great in the kingdom of heaven. For I tell you, unless your righteousness exceeds that of the scribes and Pharisees, you will never enter the kingdom of heaven.' (Mt. 5: 17-20)

In Luke 16: 17, we find, 'But it is easier for heaven and earth to pass away, than for one dot of the law to become void.'

Thus, when Jesus is regarded as a teacher of ethics, it is clear that he was more a reformer of the Hebrew tradition than a radical innovator. The Hebrew tradition had a tendency to place great emphasis on compliance with the letter of the law; the Gospel accounts of Jesus portray him as preaching against this 'righteousness of the scribes and Pharisees', championing the spirit rather than the letter of the law. Jesus was prepared to overlook Sabbath obligations, if necessary. He said: "The Sabbath was made for man not man for the Sabbath." (Mark 2: 27-28) Similarly Paul could eat food whether it was Kosher or not, depending on whether, in the given situation, it was edifying for others. (1 Cor. 10: 23-26)

As I will explain in more detail later, Jesus introduced the spirit of the law, on which 'depend all the law and the prophets' (cf. Mt. 22: 40) as one of love for God and for one's neighbour. And since obviously he was not proposing that the old teachings of 'the prophets' be discarded, he saw no need to develop a comprehensive ethical system. For Christianity morality remains a matter of revelation and discovery. Christianity thus never really broke with the Jewish conception of morality as a matter of divine law to be discovered by reading and interpreting the word of God as revealed in the scriptures. In this way, there seems to be no conflict between Jesus' position in Mt. 5: 17-20 and Luke 16: 17 and the emphasis of the rest of the Gospel and letters of Paul on the spirit of the law.

Therefore, I think Jesus' emphasis on the love of God and love of one's neighbour as the two main commandments is not to be considered as a rejection of the law and the necessity of being obedient to it. Indeed, what Jesus seems to suggest is that his people must fulfil all legal requirements, but at the same time they must realise that the whole point of this and the only way to achieve a real piety is to love God and to love one's neighbour. Compliance with the law must be done wholeheartedly and not superficially or just as a matter of formality. As St Francis de Sales has suggested,[14] some believe that perfection consists in an austere life; others

14 MacNamara, 1989, p. 11

believe that perfection consists in prayer; others in frequenting the Sacraments; others in alms giving. But, he says, they deceive themselves. Perfection consists in loving God with our whole heart. A person who loves God never does anything against His will and never omits to do anything that pleases Him. This is why St Augustine said: "Love God and do whatever you please." Therefore, there is no contradiction between the centrality of love and obedience to the law.

Christianity received the main commandments of its morality from the Old Testament.[15] In Mark 12: 28-31 we find a very important story:

'And one of the scribes came up and heard them disputing with one another, and seeing that he answered them well, asked him, "Which commandment is the first of all?" Jesus answered, "The first is, 'Hear, O Israel: The Lord our God, the Lord is one; and you shall love the Lord your God with all your heart, and with all your soul, and with all your mind, and with all your strength." The second is this, "You shall love your neighbour as your self." There is no other commandment greater than these.'

15 One has to bear in mind that, despite the fact that Christian ethics is rooted in the Old Testament and Jesus was in principle loyal to Hebrew tradition in respect to love, there is not much emphasis on the notion of love either on the Divine side or the human side in the Old Testament. It has been suggested that (T. Barrosse, 1968, pp. 1043, 1044) the Hebrew Bible prefers to use other notions, such as loyal attachment, fidelity, tenderness and active favour in order to describe God's relation to man. On the other hand, the Israelites' relationship with God (Yahweh) is described by notions such as fear, service and loyal attachment. In both cases, occasionally 'love' is spoken of. Love for fellow man as a religious duty appears only three times in the entire Hebrew Bible. In the New Testament, love represents a central notion about Divine-human relations. The notion of covenant gives place to that of paternity.

A similar story can be found in Mt. 22: 34-40 with the ending phrase, 'On these two commandments depend all the law and the prophets.' In Luke 20: 39-40 the story ends with a different question and answer. In Luke 10: 25-28 it is said that:

'And behold, a lawyer stood up to put him to the test, saying, "Teacher, what shall I do to inherit eternal life?" He said to him, "What is written in the law? How do you read?" And he answered, "You shall love the Lord your God with all your heart, and with all your soul, and with all your strength, and with all your mind; and your neighbour as your self.' And he said to him, 'You have answered right: do all this and you will live." '

Having reflected on these passages from the Gospel and their relationship with the relevant parts of the Old Testament, we find that Jesus, in response to the question raised by the scribes, quoted two separate passages from the Hebrew scriptures which were familiar to the listeners. He put them together as two sides of the same coin. He mentioned the commandment of love for neighbour along with the commandment of love for God at the level of the highest and greatest commandment, the commandment to love God.[16] Those two parts of the Old Testament are:

---

16 Paul reduces all the law to loving one's neighbour. He says, "He who loves his neighbour has fulfilled the law. The commandments, 'You shall not commit adultery, you shall not kill, you shall not steal, you shall not covet,' and any other commandments, are summed up in this sentence, 'You shall love your neighbour as yourself.' Love does no wrong to a neighbour: therefore love is the fulfilling of the law." (Rom. 13: 8-10)

"For the whole law is fulfilled in one word, 'You shall love your neighbour as yourself'." (Gal. 5: 14)

'Hear, O Israel: The Lord our God is one Lord; and you shall love the Lord your God with all your heart, and with all your soul, and with all your might.' (Deut 6: 4-5)

'You shall not hate your brother in your heart, but you shall reason with your neighbour, lest you bear sin because of him. You shall not take vengeance or bear any grudge against the sons of your own people, but you shall love your neighbour as yourself: I am the Lord.' (Leviticus 19: 17-18)

III

Love and related concepts

Having sketched the outline of the discussion about the commandment of love, let us unpack the concept of 'love' and its synonyms. There have been different definitions presented for the concept of 'love'. Every group of thinkers has emphasised some aspects of this concept. Some are rather philosophical, like the definition of love as 'an affective accord or union with what is in some way grasped as congenial'.[17]

Chervin in *Church of Love* highlights three elements of love that seem to be generally accepted. One is that love is a self-giving act. Love is not just to give *something* to the beloved, it requires you to give yourself to the beloved. For example, if a young man gives his wife many presents, but keeps *himself* withdrawn, she will become unhappy. This aspect of God's love for mankind is known by considering the fact that He has given His only Son to them. In other words, He has given Himself through His Son. On what the Church teaches about God the Father, the Catechism of the Church of England says: "The Church teaches that God the Father made me and all mankind, and that in his love he sent his Son to reconcile the world to himself."[18]

The second is that love is never static. The lover does

---

17 Johann, 1967,　p. 1039
18 *The Revised Catechism*, 1996, Q. 9

not simply give himself and then rest. Instead, love tends towards greater and greater intimacy of union. It has been suggested that 'by love one takes leave of one's self, as it were, and makes one's abode with the beloved object'.[19]

The third is that love is transforming. Love makes the lover live in the way that pleases the beloved. One's love for God transforms one to a true believer.[20]

One has to bear in mind that historically there has been a departure in the New Testament from the Hellenistic understanding of love, expressed in the Platonic concept of *eros*, to the biblical understanding of love, *agape*. Although erotic love has frequently been understood primarily as sexual desire and passion, its classical religious and philosophical meaning was 'the overriding dynamism of the soul'[21] or 'the idealistic desire to acquire the highest spiritual and intellectual good' (*Britannica*, 1997). Early Christianity took *eros* as the most sublime form of egocentricity and self-assertion and therefore the Greek New Testament did not use the word *eros* but rather the relatively rare word '*agape*'. *Agape* was translated into Latin as 'caritas' and thus appeared in English as 'charity' and, later, 'love'. In the New Testament, *agape* means the mutual love of God and man. The term necessarily extends to the love of one's fellow man – See 1 John 4: 19-21. Brett writes:

> 'Christian love is what I owe you purely because you are another person like me. There is a fundamental element of equality involved; we are to love our neighbours as ourselves.'[22]

---

19 Graham, 1939, p.22
20 See Chervin, 1973, pp. 9, 10, 19, 62
21 Johann, 1967, p. 1040
22 Brett, 1992, p. 3

It should be noted that *agape* was also used in the sense of 'love feast'. During the first century AD, Christian communities developed into self-contained units and they began to see themselves as a church. At that time they held two separate kinds of services: firstly, meetings on the model of the synagogue that were open to inquirers and believers and consisted of readings from the Jewish scriptures and, secondly, *agape*, or 'love feasts', for believers only. It was a meal of fellowship to which the poor were invited. The latter was an evening meal in which the participants shared and during which a brief ceremony, recalling the Last Supper, commemorated the Crucifixion. This was also a thanksgiving ceremony; the Greek name for it was Eucharist, meaning 'the giving of thanks'. This common meal gradually became impracticable as the Christian communities grew larger, and the Lord's Supper was thereafter observed at the conclusion of the public part of the scripture service.

A similar concept is 'charity' (a translation of the Greek word *agape*, also meaning 'love'). Charity is the highest form of love, the reciprocal love between God and man that is made manifest in unselfish love of one's fellow men. In Christian theology and ethics, charity is most eloquently shown in the life, teachings, and death of Jesus Christ.

On Christian thought about charity St Augustine writes: 'Charity is a virtue which, when our affections are perfectly ordered, unites us to God, for by it we love him.' Using this definition and others from the Christian tradition, the medieval theologians, especially St Thomas, placed charity within the theological virtues (along with faith and hope) and specified its role as 'the foundation or root' of them all. Although the controversies of the Reformation dealt more with the definition of faith than with either hope or charity, the Reformers identified the uniqueness of God's *agape* for man as unmerited love. Therefore, they required that charity, as man's love for man, be based, not upon the desirability of its object, but upon the transformation of its subject through the power of divine *agape*.

St Augustine's word for the ethical valuation that influences conduct is *amor* (love). *Amor* is the moral dynamic that impels man to action. All lesser goods are to be 'used' as means or aids toward the higher; only the highest is to be 'enjoyed' as the ultimate end on which the heart is set. The supreme good in whose fruition alone man reaches his perfection is, for St Augustine, God, whose nature is *agape*. If, then, man's love, his *amor*, can rise to the enjoyment of God, it will become a participation in the divine *agape*, love itself. God will have given Himself to men, and by sharing in His love men will love one another as He loves them, drawing from Him the power to give themselves to others.

IV

Divine love

It is obvious from what we have said up to now that in Christianity love is attributed to both God and human beings. However, there are some important differences between Divine and human love. One difference is that the former is substantive, a property, while in the latter case love is just a predicate. The reason for that is the fact that God is love, but human beings can only do love. They may be loveable and loving, but only God *is* love. This fact is clearly expressed twice in the following passage:

'He who does not love does not know God; for God is love. In this the love of God was made manifest among us, that God sent his only Son into the world, so that we might live through him... God is love, and he who abides in love abides in God, and God abides in him.' (I John 4: 8-16)

It has been argued[23] that since love is the ultimate purpose of His interaction with humanity, including the very revelation of Himself, and it is a love without measure and beyond comparison, love can be considered as the most specific characteristic of His being. Love is His nature and therefore, an appropriate name for Him.[24]

---

23 Cerini, 1992, p. 9
24 Barrosse (1967, p. 1044) makes an important comparison between

God has loved human beings 'with an everlasting love' (cf. Jer. 31: 3). God was the first to love us. We were not there yet, neither was the world created, but He already loved us. He has loved us as long as He is God and as long as He has loved Himself.

God's love for mankind is demonstrated in the whole existence and history of human beings: as individuals or as human species. His love is manifested in His creation of human beings. His love is manifested in the call of Abraham to the Sinai Covenant, in all His interventions in the history of Israel, in His constant presence in the midst of His People and in His continual re-gathering them after their every fall.

God loves human beings to the extent that, not only has He given them all they have, but also He has made everything in the world for their benefit. As St Augustine has suggested, everything on the earth or above the earth speaks to us and exhorts us to love Him, because all assure us that God has made them for love of us. This is an idea that one can easily understand from the following passage of the Psalms in the Old Testament:

'What is man that thou art mindful of him, and the son of man that thou dost care for him? Yet thou hast made him little less than God, and dost crown him with glory and honour. Thou hast given him dominion over the works of thy hands; thou hast put all things under his feet, all sheep and oxen, and also the beasts of the

different parts of the N.T. i.e. the *Synoptic Gospels*, the *Pauline Epistles* and the *Johannine writings*. I think his comparison shows that successively the emphasis on the concept of love in those three parts of the NT intensifies. It reaches its apex in the writings of St John who never uses any term other than love to describe God's beneficence towards man. Christ's Passion-Resurrection in St Paul's writings is taken to manifest Jesus' and his Father's love, while in the writings of St John it reveals that God is love.

field, the birds of the air, and the fish of the sea, whatever passes along the paths of the sea.' (Ps 8: 4-8)

God's love for man is not limited to all those beautiful creatures that He has given man. As I mentioned earlier, the Christian view is that God's love at its highest has appeared in giving Himself through His Son. According to St John, 'God so loved the world that he gave his only son.' (cf. John 3: 16)

In Christianity, the notion of God's paternal love is very significant: God's love for mankind is compared to that of a father for his children. For example, in the New Testament God is addressed as 'Our Father who art in heaven' (cf. Mt. 6: 9) and since Jesus taught his disciples to pray like this: 'Our Father who art in heaven, hallowed be thy name', this verse is considered to be a good reason to assume that God can be and wishes to be called 'Father'.[25] It is the Father in heaven who 'makes his sun rise on the evil and on the good, and sends the rain on the just and unjust.' (cf. Mt. 5: 45) God's paternal love manifests itself in His attention to the needy (cf. Mt. 6:32), in His great concern for the captives and the oppressed (cf. Luke 4: 18,19) and even in His meeting with sinners, whether searching for them (cf. Luke 15: 4-7) or confidently waiting for them in order to rejoice and happily welcome their return (cf. Luke 15: 11-32).

There is also a tendency in Christian thought to compare God's love for human beings individually or collectively to that of a bridegroom for his bride. Graham argues that such a comparison is justified according to

25 For example, see Cerini, 1992, p. 21. Lubich writes: "Jesus, so this is how you reveal it! This is how you announce the reality that I have a Father!" Ibid., cited from C.Lubich, *Diary* 1964/65 (New York, 1987), pp. 72 & 73

the scriptures and also philosophically. He believes that 'this is the closest of earthly unions'. He also says:

'Our Lord, when on earth, was pleased to suggest such a relationship Himself and the idea has become a part of Catholic tradition. One has but to recall the influence of Solomon's Song of Songs on the language of spirituality for confirmation of this.'[26]

It is important to realise that even creatures' love for God is directly in God's debt. As Graham puts it, 'the preliminaries of the great marriage between heaven and earth belong, as might be expected, to God alone. It is the part of the bridegroom to make the first advances.'[26] On how one can carry out one's duties (including loving Him) and overcome temptation and sin, the *Catechism of the Catholic Church* states: 'The preparation of man for the reception of grace is already a work of grace.' (no. 2001) *The Revised Catechism* of the Church of England writes:

'I can do these things only by the help of God and through his grace. By God's grace I mean that God himself acts in Jesus Christ to forgive, inspire, and strengthen me by his Holy Spirit.' (Q. 26 & Q. 27)

In general, one can say that, unlike our love either for God or for our fellow-human beings, which is a passive response to the beloved, divine love is both creative and active. With God it is not the case that He discerns something loveable in the beloved object; He rather grants desirable qualities to things and 'this is precisely His love for them'.[27] As St Thomas Aquinas has said, "The love of God influences and creates the goodness which is pres-

26 Graham, 1939, p.34

27 Graham, 1939, p.36

ent in things." Therefore, God does not love us because He has found some goodness in us; it is because He has loved us that we have goodness.

Thus, in Divine love we find the ideal and ultimate selfless quality. There is nothing there before His act of love, so He does not gain anything, either from the beloved, or from the love itself. God has all life and goodness within Himself and, therefore, He acquires nothing by loving us. It is impossible to suppose that He can share in or gain from what He has already got.

Naturally, the question arises as to why God should have created the world. There is a unanimous reply in Christian tradition. God created the heavens and the earth 'to show forth His own truth and goodness and beauty.'[28] We find in the proverbs that, 'The Lord hath made all things for himself.' (Proverbs xvi, 4)[29] Graham adds that 'it would be tantamount to a mortal sin in God to have made the world for any other object than subserving the absolute goodness which he is.'[30] He argues that it is the nature of what is good to communicate itself to others (*Bonum est diffusivum sui*). Experience also tells that, normally, good people are generous, selfless and able to enter the thoughts and feelings of people around them, while bad people are usually selfish, egocentric and fail to establish friendships with others and to have compassion for them.

---

28 Graham, 1939, p. 37
29 This is true according to the translation of the phrase mentioned by Graham. The standard translation seems to be "The Lord has made everything for its purpose".
30 Graham, 1939, p.38

V

Human love for God

Love is a mutual relationship between God and human beings and, indeed, it is for this relationship that He has made us. We reciprocate God's love for us, which manifests itself in His boundless bounties upon us, at the least, by loving Him. In a passage, full of insight, St Bernard writes:

'Ought He not to be loved in return, when we think who loved, whom He loved, and how much He loved? For who is He that loved? The same of whom every spirit testifies: "Thou art my God: my goods are nothing unto Thee" (Ps. 16: 2, Vulg.). And is not His love that wonderful charity which "seeketh not her own"? (1 Cor. 13: 5) But for whom was such unutterable love made manifest? The apostle tells us: "When we were enemies, we were reconciled to God by the death of His Son." (Rom. 5: 10) So it was God who loved us, loved us freely, and loved us while yet we were enemies. And how great was this love of His? St John answers: "God so loved the world that He gave His only-begotten Son, that whosoever believeth in Him should not perish, but have everlasting life." (John 3:16)'[31]

Chiara Lubich, the founder of the Focolare Movement, writes about her spiritual experience and that of her companions:

31 Bernard, 1937, Chapter 1

51

'The dignity to which he raised us seemed to us so sublime, and the possibility to love him in return seemed so high and undeserved, that we used to repeat: "It's not that we should say: we must love God, but rather: Oh, that we can love you, Lord… that we can love you with this little heart of ours!" '[32]

Love for God has no limit. As St Bernard said, "The measure of love due to Him is immeasurable love." The reason is that our love for God, who is infinite and immeasurable, who loved us first and without any self-interest, cannot be limited.

Of course, human love for God has different levels. As we saw earlier, in several biblical passages Jesus asked to love the Lord your God 'with all your heart, and with all your soul, and with all your mind, and with all your strength.' This is the aim of the mystical journey. Love for God may intensify to such a degree that it occupies all the heart of the lover to the extent that he no longer thinks of himself or anything else other than God.

In Christianity, love for God is believed to be universal, i.e. practised by all creatures. While addressing God, St Augustine pointed out the same fact. He said: "O God, Who art loved knowingly or unknowingly by everything capable of loving." Explaining the same point, Graham argues that all creatures, including human beings, depend for their existence on God and, therefore, they must be conceived as loving God, stretching out their hands towards Him in 'silent acknowledgement of His act of creation.'[33] Then he adds that there is another sense of loving God, which is exclusive to human beings. Human

32 C. Lubich, May They All Be One, p. 24. Cited in Cerini, 1992, p. 38

beings are able to love God expressly and consciously. This love, of course, comes after a proportionate understanding of God. We will see in the next chapter that there is another view that belongs to those Muslim mystics and philosophers who acknowledge some conscious love of God in all beings, of course, preceded by the proportionate understanding of God.

To love God does not require us to abandon other things. It is true that closeness to God in a sense demands us to withdraw from creatures, including even ourselves, but this is only to find that nothing can stand as a partner to God, independent of his mercy. Everything of value is restored to us in God. In other words, 'Nothing noble or of good report has to be finally abandoned for charity's sake.'[34] In his *Confessions*, St Augustine makes the same point beautifully:

'But what do I love, when I love thee? Not beauty of bodies, not the fair harmony of time, nor the brightness of the light, so gladsome to our eyes, nor sweet melodies of varied songs, nor the fragrant smell of flowers, and ointments, and spices.... None of these I love, when I love my God; and yet I love a kind of light, and melody, and fragrance, and meat, and embracement, when I love my God, the light, melody, fragrance, meat, embracement of my inner man: where there shineth unto my soul, what space cannot contain... This is which I love, when I love my God.' (X, vi, 8)

33 Graham, 1939, p. 16
34 Graham, 1939, p. 60

VI

Human love for fellow-humans

As I mentioned earlier, human love for God extends to the neighbour, to fellow human beings. This love is universal and includes even sinners, non-Christians and enemies. Now let us study love for sinners, non-Christians and enemies in more details.

Some of the important phrases of the New Testament (1 John 4: 7 - 5: 4) speak of the necessity of love for fellow Christians. In fact, the practice of love of neighbour within the inner circle of the disciples was a conspicuous characteristic of the early Church. Christian congregations and, above all, small fellowships and sects, have stood out throughout the centuries because of the fact that within their communities love of neighbour was highly developed in the form of personal pastoral care, social welfare, and help in all situations of life.

Christian love, however, is not limited to any special class or group of people. On the contrary, the new factor in the Christian ethic was that it crossed all social and religious barriers and saw a neighbour in every suffering human being. Neighbourly love has to be fulfilled without 'partiality' (James 2: 9). In Luke's version of the famous story in which the commandment of love is described the lawyer asks Jesus: "Who is my neighbour?" In response Jesus tells the tale of the Good Samaritan. In this story the neighbour is a stranger, an unexpected person (in fact, someone despised) who does not belong to the same community. (Luke 10: 29-37)

On the universality of love, Chiara Lubich says: "It is a love that knows how to welcome back the neighbour who has gone astray – whether this is a friend, a brother, a sister or a stranger – and it forgives this person an infinite number of times. It is a love that rejoices more over a sinner who repents than over a thousand righteous people."[35] She adds that this love 'does not measure and will not be measured'. This love is 'abundant', 'universal' and 'active'.

The universality of the Christian command to love is most strongly expressed in its demand to love one's enemies. Jesus himself said: "You have heard that it was said, 'You shall love your neighbour and hate your enemies.' But I say to you, 'Love your enemies and pray for those who persecute you, so that you may be sons of your Father who is in heaven; for he makes his sun rise on the evil and on the good, and sends rain on the just and on the unjust.'" (Mt. 5: 43-45) Elsewhere we find that he said: "But I say to you that hear, 'Love your enemies, do good to those who hate you, bless those who curse you, pray for those who abuse you. To him who strikes you on the cheek, offer the other also; and from him who takes away your coat do not withhold even your shirt.'" (Luke 6: 27-29)

Therefore, a real Christian loves his enemies. Indeed, as Clément suggests,[36] the criterion of the depth of one's spiritual progress is nothing other than the ability to love one's enemies. The following story shows the importance of love (in this case, love for enemies) and its superiority to fear and hope. John Climacus in *The Ladder of Divine Perfection* writes:

35 C. Lubich, *Meditations* (London, 1989), pp. 66, 67
36 O. Clément 1993, p. 271

55

'One day I saw three monks insulted and humili-
ated in the same way at the same moment. The first
felt he had been cruelly hurt; he was distressed but
managed not to say anything. The second was happy
for himself but grieved for the one who had insulted
him. The third thought only of the harm suffered by
his neighbour, and wept with the most ardent compassion. The first was prompted by fear; the second
was urged on by the hope of reward; the third was
moved by love.'[37]

Love for one's neighbour in Christianity has several
typical characteristics, like equality, a corporate attitude
and a co-operative nature.

This characteristic of equality is well expressed in
what has already been quoted from Brett: "Christian
love is what I owe you purely because you are another
person like me." Because of this fundamental element
of equality, Christian ethics does not base its norms on
social, biological, psychological, physiological, intellectual, or educational differences and levels but on an
understanding and treatment of human beings as created in the image of God.

The new element of the Christian ethic is the found-
ing of the individual ethic in a corporate ethic, in the
understanding of the fellowship of Christians as the
body of Christ. The individual believer is not understood as a separate individual who has found a new
spiritual and moral relationship with God but as a 'living stone', as a living cell in the body of Christ in which
the powers of the Kingdom of God are already work-
ing. St Peter wrote to the exiles of the Dispersion in Pon-

37 Cited in Clément, 1993, p. 271

tus, Galatia, Cappadocia, Asia, and Bithynia: 'Come to him, to that living stone, rejected by men but in God's sight chosen and precious; and like living stones be yourselves built into a spiritual house, to be a holy priesthood, to offer spiritual sacrifices acceptable to God through Jesus Christ.' (1 Peter 2: 4, 5)

And its co-operative nature we see in the understanding that Christian love is not just a sentiment; it should be accompanied with benevolent acts and steps to put an end to the sufferings of the other party. Love is not just good will or a warm feeling. Love is practical, time consuming and costly. Gilleman says: "Christ's love assumes man's soul and body. Our spiritual charity must embody itself in deeds, in corporate works of mercy (Mt. 25: 35-45) and social service (Acts 4: 32-37; 6: 1)."[38] In other words, Christian spirituality is not just inward looking or upward looking. As Brett puts it, "It must also be outward-looking concerned with the neighbour, if it is to be complete."[39] In the letter to the twelve tribes in the Dispersion, St James wrote:

'What does it profit, my brethren, if a man says he has faith but has not works? Can his faith save him? If a brother or sister is ill-clad and in lack of daily food, and one of you says to them, "Go in peace, be warmed and filled," without giving them the things needed for the body, what does it profit? So faith by itself, if it has no works, is dead.' (James 2: 14-17)

Therefore, Christian love has to be expressed both in attitudes and actions. Action must be grounded in love

38 Gilleman, 1967, p. 1045
39 Brett, 1992, p. 3

and love must be expressed in action. The realisation of Christian love leads to the peculiar exchange of gifts and suffering, of exaltation and humiliations, of defeat and victory; the individual is able, through personal sacrifice and suffering, to contribute to the development of the whole. All forms of ecclesiastical, political and social communities of Christianity are founded on this basic idea of the fellowship of believers as the body of Christ.

Thus, in Christianity love plays an essential and crucial role in both theology and ethics. God Himself is love and creates the world out of love. God who is love sends His Son to redeem man and to call man, made in His image, to a share in His life. The Father shows His unique love for the Son, passing on to him His own glory and the Son shows his love for the Father by obeying His command to show supreme love for the disciples by his Resurrection. The disciples show their love for the Son by obeying his command to love one another self-sacrificingly like the Son himself. In general, man's fundamental task is to exercise generous love, *agape*, and to promote God's kingdom on earth. Man has to work for an ever-fuller presence of God in the world He made.

Part 3

Love in Islamic Ethics

I

God's love as the highest reason for creation

The concept of love is one of the most important concepts in Islamic philosophy, theology, mysticism and ethics; indeed, in some aspects, it plays the most crucial role. For example, in defining the Islamic point of view of the relation between God and the whole universe in general, and between God and mankind in particular, love has the most significant place. In this chapter, my main concern is to explain the place of love in Islamic ethics, but prior to that I have to elaborate on the concept of love in the whole Islamic world-view.

In early *kalam* (Islamic theology) a heated debate started on the purpose behind God's creations and acts. Some theologians thought that the attribution of reason or purpose to His deeds leads to the assumption that God is in need of His creatures and He creates them to meet some needs, just like a human being who, say, works to earn money, or studies to learn. However the dominant view, especially among those who have had a more rationalistic approach, has always been that God is the Wise One (*hakim*), so whatever He does is for some exactly and carefully pre-studied purposes. He never does something arbitrarily or in vain. It is asserted in the Qur'an that, 'What! Did you then think that We had created you in vain...?' (23: 115)

Of course, it is clear that God Himself does not gain

anything from His creatures, nor from His act of creation. This is not only because He is completely free from any sort of need, but also because it is logically impossible that a given effect would have any type of influence on its (existential) cause. Whatever the effect has, is received from the cause and it would be circular to suppose it otherwise. God has not created the universe to gain some benefits for Himself, but rather to give benefits. A popular Persian poem says: "I have not created the world to gain some benefits, I have created the world to show people my generosity."

There is a famous divine saying (*hadith qudsi*) which can probably be found in all books written about the goal of creation in Islam. According to this *hadith*, God says: "I was a hidden treasure; I loved to be known. Hence I created the world so that I would be known."[40] (e.g. Majlesi, 1983, Vol. 87, p. 344) The Arabic original term for 'love' is derived from the root *hubb*, which means to like or to love. *Hubb* is a general concept that can be applied to simple things, such as preferring some types of food, which in English could be translated as 'like'. Or it can refer to the most important things in one's life, such as the intense desire for a person or an ideal, to the extent that one might even be ready to be destroyed in order to please the beloved or secure the ideal. *Hubb* in such cases can be translated as 'love'. There is another term in the Islamic culture which is sometimes used in Arabic and more commonly in Persian to mean intense love, *'ishq*. There is also *wudd* which means mostly friendship and affection.

Thus, a question arises: why did God love to be known? Certainly, God has no desire for fame. The purpose behind

---

40 e.g. Majlesi, 1983, Vol. 87, p. 344

His love to be known is understandable by considering the fact that God is Wise, Compassionate and Omnipotent. He creates the universe, and particularly human beings, to give them the maximum grace and perfection they are capable of receiving. Of course, the perfection of any kind of being is decided by the degree of its similarity or closeness to God, and the most important factors in this are love of God, and prior to that, knowledge of God, since there can be no love without knowing the beloved subject.

II

God's love for Himself

Since the reason for loving something is nothing other than the apprehension by the lover of the beauty and perfection or, more generally, the pleasantness of the beloved, the greatest possible love is certainly the love of God for Himself. God is the most beautiful and the most perfect being and His apprehension of Himself is also the best apprehension, so His love for Himself and His joy are the most intense ones. Avicenna writes:

'The necessarily existent (*Wajib al-wujud*) that has the highest perfection, beauty and brightness and perceives of Himself as so with a complete perception ... is in Himself the greatest lover and the greatest beloved and has the greatest joy...'[41]

Elsewhere he says:

'The being that has the greatest joy in respect to something is the First (*al-Awwal*) in respect to Himself, since He has the greatest understanding and has the greatest perfection.'[42]

Sadr ud-din al-Shirazi, known as Mulla Sadra and the founder of the school of a*l-hikmah al-muta'aliyah*, makes the same point:

---

41 Avicenna, 1956, p. 369
42 Avicenna, 1375 A.H., Vol. 3, p. 359

'Love is caused by what is received or will be received from the beloved. The higher goodness and more intense existence the more deserving for being loved and the greater love for goodness. Now the being, which is free from potentiality and contingency, due to its ultimate goodness, has the ultimate level of being loved and the ultimate level of loving. Therefore, His love for Himself is the most perfect love and the most loyal one.'[43]

He also adds that, since God is simple (not compound) and Divine attributes are not additional (or accidental) to His essence in existence (the idea which is greatly accepted by Muslim philosophers and the majority of theologians and known as the unity of His essence and His attributes), His love is identical to His essence. In this way, one can justifiably say that He is love as He is knowledge and life.

---

43 al-Shirazi, 1378 A.H., Vol. 2, p.274

III

God's love for creatures

God's love for the world in general, and human beings in particular is unanimously believed and emphasised by all Muslims. Indeed, one of God's names is *al-Wadud*, 'He who loves'. This is in addition to those names which imply His love for creatures, such as *al-Rahman* and *al-Rahim*, meaning the all-Compassionate, the all-Merciful. Every chapter of the Qur'an, except chapter 9, (which starts with verses about warning pagans) begins with the phrase: 'In the Name of God, the all-Compassionate, the all-Merciful'. Yet the number of repetitions of this phrase in the Qur'an is equal to the number of chapters, i.e. 114, since in chapter 27 this phrase occurs twice. It is noteworthy that although one of the things attributed to God in Islam is wrath (*ghadab*), its application is much more limited compared to His mercy and love for His creatures. Indeed, His wrath is only for those who deliberately disbelieve or commit evil actions. This is an idea that all Muslims agree on, and is clearly expressed in many sources. I would like here just to mention only one profound statement. In a well-known prayer, *Jushan al-Kabir*, God is addressed as the one 'whose mercy has preceded His wrath'.

As we will see later, this wrath or anger is also out of His love and mercy. If His love or mercy did not exist He would not care at all. It is like a father who becomes angry with his son when he does something wrong. It is because he has care and concern for his son and his entire family, because he wants his son to correct his behaviour and set a lesson for other children not to copy that wrong act.

God has different levels or degrees of love for His creatures. One is His general and encompassing love that includes all beings. If there were no such love nothing would be brought into being. This love includes even wrongdoers, since they also manifest or represent some stages of goodness in their essence and this is that aspect of their being which is loved by God, though it might be overwhelmed by the demonic aspect of their characters and therefore ultimately they may be hated.

A higher level of Divine love is His love for true believers, those who believe in Him and do good deeds. Those are the people 'He loves and who love Him' (5: 54). In the Qur'an, we find that God loves 'the doers of justice' (5: 42; 8: 60; 9: 49), 'those who purify themselves' (9: 108), 'the pious' (3: 76; 9: 4 & 7), 'those who do good (to others)' (5: 13 & 93; 3: 134 & 148; 2: 195), 'those who trust (Him)' (4: 35), 'the patient'(3: 146) and 'those who repent very much and purify themselves'(2: 222).

It is noteworthy that in the Qur'an in many cases God's displeasure is described, not by focusing on His hatred, but rather indirectly by phrases, such as 'God does not love any ungrateful (or unbelieving) sinner' (2:276), 'God does not love the unjust' (3: 57 & 1140), 'surely, God does not love him who is proud, boastful' (4: 36) and 'surely God does not love him who is treacherous, sinful' (4: 107).

IV

God's love for perfect human beings

According to Islam, the highest level of Divine love for any creature is His love for perfect human beings such as prophets. The Prophet Muhammad has a special place in this regard. One of his best-known titles is *Habib Ullah*, which means the beloved of God. In a famous Divine saying God addresses the Prophet, "If thou were not, I would not have created the heavens." As S.H. Nasr and many others have indicated, "Muslim saints over the centuries have seen in the love of God for the Prophet and in his love for God the prototype of all love between man and his creator."[44]

---

44 Nasr, 1989, p. 321

V

Human love

Similar to what we saw earlier in the case of Divine love, human love for God, for His creation, for good deeds, and for each other plays a crucial role in the Islamic world-view, especially in theology, mysticism and ethics. Indeed, love for the truths embodied in religion builds up the faith. Though faith, for Muslim theologians, is based on knowledge of religious facts, it is not reducible to that knowledge. There might be people who have knowledge of religious facts but who still do not commit themselves to any faith. Faith and belief only come when a person voluntarily commits himself to acceptance of articles of faith and does not refuse to follow them. In other words, the faith is there only when one loves the religious beliefs and not just when one comes to know them. The Qur'an says:

'And they denied them (Divine signs or miracles) unjustly and proudly while their soul was certain about them.' (27: 14)

The prototype of those who know very well but refuse to practise what they have known is *Iblis*, the great Satan. According to Islamic sources, *Iblis* does whatever he does out of arrogance and selfishness, not out of ignorance.

Thus, a person becomes faithful and a believer only

when he has respect and love for certain facts, i.e. articles
of faith. We read in a famous *hadith* that the Prophet
Muhammad asked his companions about 'the firmest
handhold of faith'. They suggested different things like
prayer and *hajj*. When they could not give the appropriate
answer, the Prophet said:

'The firmest handhold of faith is to love for the sake
of God and to hate for the sake of God, to befriend
God's friends and to renounce His enemies.'[45]

The same idea is emphasised by Imams of the
Household of the Prophet. For example, Fudayl ibn
Yasar, a disciple, asked Imam Sadiq whether love and
hatred derive from faith. Imam replied: "Is faith anything but love and hate?"[46] The same *hadith* is narrated
from Imam Baqir. It is also narrated that Imam Baqir
said: 'Faith is love and love is faith.'[47]

An overall study of the Qur'an and narrations
(*hadiths*) shows that in the Islamic view love, either in its
Divine form or in human form, belongs to the precious
and valuable things only insofar they are precious and
valuable. The result is firstly, that the degrees of love
that different things deserve or receive differ according
to their merits, and secondly, that anything which is in conflict with those precious and valuable things or prevents
their realisation should be hated. For example, if justice
is to be loved, injustice should be hated; or if a person
who tells the truth is to be loved, a person who lies

---

45 Al-Kulayni, 1397 A.H., *Kitab al-Iman wal-Kufr*, "Bab al-Hubb fi Allah
wal-Bughd fi Allah", no. 6, p.126

46 Ibid., no. 5 , p. 125

47 Al-Majlisi, 1983, *Kitab al-Iman wal-Kufr*, "Bab al-Hubb fi Allah wal-
Bughd fi Allah", lxvi, p. 238

should be hated. Of course, in respect of the other aspects of their character and their deeds, the situation might be different. A single person might be loved or praised for something and at the same time he might be hated or blamed for something else.

In contrast with some other faiths, one aspect of love in Islam is that it is usually considered along with 'hatred (of evil) for the sake of God'. One has to love for the sake of God and to hate for the sake of God. There is a tendency among some people to think that there should be no hate at all. These people assume that excellence and nobility of character and 'being sociable' consist in having everyone as a friend. Certainly Islam recommends Muslims to love people and optimise compassionate and sincere relationships with them, even if they do not believe in Islam or in God. However, it is not feasible for a person who has principles in his life and has devoted his life to realise sacred values to be indifferent to evil and oppressive deeds of wrongdoers and make friendship with everybody. Such a person certainly will have some enemies. There are always good and bad people in society. There are fair people and despotic people. Good and bad are two opposite poles. Attraction towards the good is not possible without repulsion from the bad.

When two human beings are attracted to each other and they wish to become friends, we should look for a reason for that. The reason is nothing other than similarity and resemblance. Unless there is a similarity between these two persons, they cannot attract one another and move towards friendship with each other. Rumi in his *Mathnavi* mentions two fine stories that illustrate this fact. One story is that once a very wise and well-known Greek physician asked his disciples for some medicine for himself. His disciples were shocked. They said: "O, Master!

This medicine is for the treatment of madness, but you are the wisest person that we know." The master replied: "On my way here, I met a mad person. When he saw me he stopped and smiled. Now, I am afraid that he must have found some similarity between me and himself; otherwise he would not have enjoyed looking at me." The other story relates to another wise man who saw a raven that had developed an affection for a stork. They perched together and flew together! The wise man could not understand how two birds of two different species that had no similarity either in shape or in colour with each other could be friends. He went close and discovered that both of them had only one leg.

> *That wise man said: "I saw companionship*
> *Between a raven and a stork.*
> *Amazed I was, I examined their condition*
> *To see what sign of commonality I could find.*
> *So up I crept, and, lo and behold!*
> *I saw that both of them were lame."*

In Islam, there has been much emphasis on the necessity of promoting brotherhood and friendship with people of faith and people of good will, and at the same time combating against evil, corruption and oppressors. Of course, in Islam love is universal and the Prophet of Islam was not sent, 'save as a mercy unto all beings' (The Qur'an 21: 107). Therefore, even fighting against those who do wrongs and injustice should be out of love. It is an act of genuine love for mankind as a whole and even, say for a murderer such as Hitler, to fight against him, to punish him and, if necessary, to destroy him. Otherwise, he would do more crimes and would degrade himself more and more and would suffer much more severe punishments in this world and hereafter.

There is a beautiful story that once an oppressive ruler asked a pious person to pray for him. In response, that pious person asked God not to let him live anymore. That oppressor was shocked and said: "I asked you to pray for me and not against me!" He replied: "This is exactly what I did. It is much better for you and, of course, for the people as well, that your life becomes shorter. You will then have less chance to add to your crimes and people will have more chance to rest."

A rational and intelligent love is one that involves the good and interest of mankind and not a limited number of people. One can do many things to bring good to individuals or groups which bring evil to society or mankind as a whole. For example, if a judge releases a guilty criminal he might have done something good to that person, but a great harm has been inflicted upon society and the ideal of justice. One should not let one's affections hide the truth. If our beloved child needs an injection or an operation we should not let our love and passions for him prevent us from doing so.

According to Islam, love has to be enlightened. Sacred love is a love which is realistic and insightful. It has been a common theme in the ethical teaching of great Muslim preachers and Sufi masters that one should not let one's love for something or someone make him negligent of the whole truth. The reason for this emphasis is that love naturally tends to make the lover 'blind and deaf'. If you love someone it is very unlikely that you will have an impartial view, unless the love is directed by reason. This is why even Sufi Muslims try not to be overwhelmed by love. Siraj ed-Din writes:

> 'The Sufi has no choice but to be vigilant, observant, and discerning, to put everything in its rightful place, and to give everything its due. ... It is in virtue

of this perspective that Sufism is a way of knowledge rather than a way of love. As such it tends to repudiate partialities which the perspective of love necessarily condones and even encourages.'[48]

---

48 Siraj ed-Din, 1989, p. 234

VI

Human love for God

According to Islam, the minimum expectation from believers is that God should have the first place in their heart, in the sense that no other love may override one's love for God; God should be the highest and foremost object of love. The Qur'an says:

'Say: If your father or your sons or your brethren or your wives or your kinsfolk or the property you have acquired or the commerce you fear may slacken or the dwellings which you love – if these are dearer to you than God and His Apostle and striving in His way, then wait till God brings about His command; God does not guide the transgressing people.' (9: 24)

This verse clearly indicates that love for God has to be superior to love for whatever else one may come to love in life. This superiority shows itself when love for God and for His religion comes into conflict with love for personal belongings. In this case, a believer should be able to sacrifice his personal favourite things for the sake of God. For example, if God asks us to give our lives to protect innocent lives or our territorial integrity or the like, we should not let our love of the easy life or being with the family and so on prevent us from striving in His way.

Therefore, a believer is not a person who just loves God. A believer is a person whose love for God is the highest and strongest love he has. Elsewhere, the Qur'an says:

> 'Yet there are some people who adopt rivals instead of God, whom they love just as they (should) love God. Those who believe are firmer in their love of God ...' (2: 165)

Why should one love God? According to Islam, one reason for loving God lies in the fact that God is the most precious, the most perfect and the most beautiful being that a man can ever conceive, and, therefore, man, because his nature aspires to beauty and perfection, loves God.

Many Muslim scholars, especially mystics, have asserted that everybody feels in his heart a great love for God without necessarily being aware of it. They argue that even unbelievers, who are just pursuing secular aims or ideals, love and worship God in what they take to be *the ultimate good*. For example, those who want to possess power want to have the ultimate power. Becoming mayor, or even president will never satisfy them. Even if they were in control of the whole globe they would then think about controlling other planets. Nothing in the world can set their hearts at rest. As soon as people achieve their ideals, they realise that it is not sufficient and they seek for more. Islamic mystics, such as Ibn Arabi, inspired by the Qur'an, believe that the reason behind this phenomenon is that everybody in fact is seeking the ultimate good, that is, God. The Qur'an says: "O man! Surely you strive (to attain) to your Lord, a hard striving until you meet Him." (84: 6) However, the fact is that many people make a mistake in recognising what is the highest good. Some might take money as the highest good or, in other words, as their god. Others might take political power as their god, and so on. The Qur'an says: "Have you seen him who takes his low desires for his god?" (25: 43; 45: 23)

If it happens that they reach what they have set up as their ideal, their innate love for God, the highest good, will remain unanswered and so they will feel unhappy and frustrated. Ibn Arabi says:

'Nothing other than God has ever been loved. It is God who has manifested Himself in whatever is beloved in the eyes of those who love. There is no being except that it loves. Thus, the whole universe loves and is loved and all these go back to Him just as nothing has ever been worshipped other than Him, since whatever a servant (of God) has ever worshipped has been because of wrong imagination of deity in it; otherwise it would have never been worshipped. God, the most High, says (in the Qur'an): 'and your Lord has commanded not to worship but Him.' (17: 23) This is the case with love as well. No one has ever loved anything other than his Creator. However, He, the most High, has hidden Himself from them under the love for Zaynab, Su'ad, Hind, Layla, dunya (this world), money, social position and all other beloved subjects in the universe.'[49]

Ibn Arabi adds that: "Mystics have never heard any poem or praise or the like but about Him (and they saw Him) beyond veils."[49]

The other reason for loving God is to reciprocate His love and blessings. There is a rich literature in Islamic sources on different aspects and manifestations of God's love and favour for all human beings, including, in a

---

49 Ibn Arabi, 1994, Vol. 2., p. 326

sense, wrongdoers and those who disbelieve in Him. Human beings love whoever does good to them, and they appreciate such favour and benevolence and feel obliged to be thankful. The Prophet said:

'Love God because He has done good to you and He has bestowed favours upon you.'[50]

According to Islamic *hadiths*, God said to both Moses and David: "Love Me and endear Me to My people." [51] Then in response to their question as to how to endear Him to the people, God said: "Remind them about My favours and bounties, for they do not recall My favours without the feeling of gratitude." [52](Ibid.)
In a mystical prayer, known as the Whispered of the Thankful, Imam Sajjad says:

'My God, the uninterrupted flow of Thy graciousness has distracted me from thanking Thee!

The flood of Thy bounty has rendered me incapable of counting Thy praises!

The succession of Thy kind acts has diverted me from mentioning Thee in laudation!

The continuous rush of Thy benefits has thwarted me from spreading the news of Thy gentle favours!'

Then he adds:

'My God, my thanksgiving is small before Thy great boons, and my praise and news-spreading shrink beside Thy generosity toward me!

Thy favours have wrapped me in the robes of the lights of faith, and the gentlenesses of Thy goodness

50 al-Daylami, 1370 A.H., p. 226
51 al-Majlisi, 1983, Vol.8, p.351 & Vol. 14, p. 38; (my translation)
52 Ibid.

have let down over me delicate curtains of might!

Thy kindnesses have collared me with collars not to be moved and adorned me with neck-rings not to be broken!

Thy boons are abundant, my tongue is too weak to count them!

Thy favours are many, my understanding falls short of grasping them, not to speak of exhausting them!

So how can I achieve thanksgiving?'[53]

A believer who has started his spiritual journey towards God first comes to recognise God's blessings upon him in the fact that God is providing him with lots of support and help that enables him to act. Having continued his journey and been equipped with a mystical view of the world, he will realise that indeed every good thing comes from God Himself. We read in the Qur'an: 'Whatever benefit comes to you (O man!), it is from God, and whatever misfortune befalls you, it is from yourself.' (4: 79) There is no reason to think otherwise. The reason for inflicting unjust suffering can be one of the following things or a combination of them:

Lack of power: A person who oppresses others may do so because he wants to gain something from it, or because he cannot prevent himself from doing something harmful to others.

Lack of knowledge: A person may even have good intentions of benevolence, but due to lack of information or making wrong conclusions may do something that harms the recipient.

53 Chittick, 1987, pp. 242 & 243

Hatred and malevolence: A person may be able to do good deeds and may also know how to do them, but he still fails to do so, because he is not kind enough to do so, or even worse, because he hates the recipient and wants to satisfy his anger and wrath by inflicting pain on the recipient.

Muslim thinkers argue that God never does anything unjust or harmful to His servants, since there are none of the above reasons for being so: He is the all-Powerful, the all-Knowing and the all-Merciful.

Thus, the picture of God in Islam is the picture of one who is love, the all-Merciful, the all-Compassionate and the all-Benevolent, one who loves His creatures more than they may ever love Him or themselves, one whose anger and wrath is out of love and preceded by love. There seems to be no difference among Muslims in believing in God who is love, though they might vary in the amount of emphasis that they put on this aspect of the Islamic world-view compared to others. In general, it might be said that Muslim mystics and Sufis are more concerned with this aspect of Islam than Muslim philosophers, and Muslim philosophers in turn are more concerned than theologians. But, as mentioned before, there is no disagreement on seeing God as the one who is love, the all-Merciful and the all-Compassionate. We read in the Qur'an that in response to Moses' request for the good life in this world and hereafter, God said: "(As for) My chastisement, I will afflict with it whom I please, and My mercy encompasses all things." (7: 156) We find in the Qur'an that a group of angels who bear the Divine throne pray: "Our Lord! Thou embracest all things in mercy and knowledge, therefore forgive those who repent and follow Thy way and save them from the punishment of Hell." (40: 7)

Although God's love is not arbitrary and may vary from one subject to another, depending on their merits, He loves all creatures. His love for wrongdoers and those who have turned their backs on Him is so great that it completely surpasses their expectations. The emphasis on this aspect of Divine love constitutes a considerable part of Islamic literature, including Qur'anic verses, *hadiths* and even poems. For example, we read in the Qur'an:

'Say: O my servants! Who have acted extravagantly against themselves, do not despair of the mercy of God; Surely God forgives the faults altogether; surely He is the Forgiving, the Merciful.' (39: 53)

The idea of repentance is one of the key concepts in this regard. In many verses of the Qur'an, God speaks of the constant possibility of repenting and returning to Him, since He is the Forgiving. He says:

'But whoever repents after his iniquity and reforms (himself), then surely God will return to him (mercifully); surely God is Forgiving, Merciful.' (5: 39)

The Qur'an also refers to the fact that God not only forgives those who seek forgiveness, but also He may change their wrong deeds to good deeds. On those who repent and believe and do good deeds, the Qur'an says: "… these are they of whom God changes the evil deeds to good ones; and God is Forgiving, Merciful." (25: 70)

It is interesting that in the Qur'an, God is not presented just as the one who accepts the sincere repentance of his servants and returns to them when they return to him. Indeed, it is God Himself that first attends to His servants who have broken, in one way or another, their relation-

ship of servitude with God, but still have love for goodness and truth in their hearts (i.e. their hearts are not
sealed). God returns to such servants and then they repent
and return to Him, and then God returns to them to forgive
them. Therefore, as S.H. Tabatabai, the author of *Al-Mizan*
on the interpretation of the Qur'an in 20 volumes, notifies,
every repentance and return of a wrongdoing servant is
accompanied by two returns of God: the first return gives
that person the ability for voluntary repentance and the
second return is His forgiveness after the person has
repented. The fact is clearly suggested by the Qur'an:

> '... they knew it for certain that there was no refuge
> from God but in Him; then He turned to them (merci-
> fully) that they might turn (to Him); Surely God is the
> oft-returning (to mercy), the Merciful.' (9: 118)

According to Islamic mysticism, one's knowledge of
God as the most beautiful and perfect being and the
source of all good things, and one's love for God who is
love and mercy, becomes so strong and so encompassing
that it will occupy all one's heart. At the same time,
knowledge of one's weakness and deficiencies in front
of God gets so intense and deep that finally one will feel
emptiness and nothingness. As such a person loses his
egocentricity and becomes selfless, he will be identifiable
with every type of goodness. From nothingness, one
reaches the position of 'everythingness'. He will feel no
limitation or restriction. In a well-known *hadith*, we read
that 'Servitude to God is a substance, whose essence is
lordship.' (Shomali, 1996, p. 32) A pure servant of God
whose will is merged into His will is able to bring about
extraordinary deeds.

Sheikh Mahmud Shabistari in his *Sa'adat-Nameh* has
a beautiful description of what he takes to be different

stages of the spiritual journey towards God. He says:

'The service and worship of God
Is a dictate of the Merciful
To every creature: man and jinn alike.
And yet this order takes to task
The most elect, as God has said:
"I did not create the jinn and men for aught but
    they should worship Me." (the Qur'an, 51: 56)
Through worship man is brought to prayer;
From prayer to mystical thought, and then from
    thought
The flame of gnosis leaps, until he sees
The truth with contemplation's inner eye.
Such wisdom comes from altruistic love
    [or kindness]:
The latter is its fruit, the first the bough.
At last comes Love which ousts all else:
Love undoes all sense of 'two';
Love makes all One,
Until no 'mine'
Nor 'thine'
Remain.' [54]

Suhrawardi in *On the Reality of Love* elaborates his view on the spiritual journey. He believes that this journey and its states and stations arise from virtue (*husn*), love (*mihr*) and reflective sadness (*huzn*). He relates virtue to the knowledge of God and love to the knowledge of self. Sadness is the outcome of the knowledge of what was not and then was. Suhrawardi believes that knowledge of the self leads to the discovery that the self is divine and this results in loving God and having mys-

---

54 Cited from Lewisohn, 1995, pp. 231 & 232

tical experiences. It is indeed a Qur'anic idea which is clearly and greatly emphasised by *Sunnah* that there is a necessary relation between knowing one's self and knowing one's Lord. For example, the Prophet Muhammad said: "Whoever knows himself has known his Lord."[55] Suhrawardi believes that sadness is caused by reflection on the created order which signifies separation of man and his departure from his original abode.[56]

According to Islam, love for God is very active and manifests itself in all aspects of one's life. It shapes all one's love and hatred. It also shapes one's behaviour with others and with one's self. In the well-known *hadith* of *nawafil* (meaning non-compulsory good deeds) we read: 'Nothing makes My servants closer to Me compared to the performance of obligatory deeds, *wajibat*. My servant constantly gets close to Me by *nawafil* till I love him. When I love him, then I shall be his ears with which he listens, his eyes with which he sees, his tongue with which he speaks, and his hands with which he holds: if he calls Me, I shall answer him, and if he asks Me, I shall give him.'[57]

A sincere lover has no power to disobey the beloved person or to refuse his wishes. Imam Ja'far al-Sadiq said: "Do you disobey God and pretend you love Him? This is amazing. If you were true you would have obeyed Him, for the lover is submissive before the one whom he loves."[58] We read in the Qur'an:

'O you who believe! Whoever from among you turns back from his religion, then God will bring a

---

55 For a discussion on self-knowledge (ma'rifat al-nafs), See Shomali, 1996

56 For a discussion on his view in this regard see Razavi, 1997, especially p.680.

57 al- Kulayni, 1397 A.H., 'Vol. 4.' p. 54

58 Cited from Mutahhari, 1985, Ch. 6

people, He shall love them and they shall love Him, lowly before the believers, mighty against the unbelievers, they shall strive hard in God's way and shall not fear the censure of any censurer.' (5: 54)

The history of Islam is full of memories of those who embodied a sincere and overwhelming love for God and His religion. One of those who devoted himself wholeheartedly to Islam was Bilal al-Habashi, a black slave. The pagans of Mecca subjected him to torture asking him to mention names of their idols and express his belief in them and disbelieve in Islam. They tormented him under the burning sun by laying him on scorching stones and putting heavy rocks on his chest. Abu Bakr, a rich companion of the Prophet, was passing by when he heard the cry of Bilal. He went close and advised him to hide his belief, but Bilal was not prepared to do so, since 'love was ever rebellious and deadly'. Illustrating the event, Rumi says:

> *Bilal was devoting his body to the thorns:*
> *His master was flogging him by way of correction,*
> [Saying:] *"Why dost thou celebrate Ahmad* [the other name of the Prophet]?
> *Wicked slave, thou disbelievest in my religion!"*
> *He was beating him in the sun with thorns*
> [While] *he cried vauntingly "One!"*
> *Till when Siddiq* [Abu Bakr] *was passing in that neighbourhood,*
> *Those cries of 'One!' reached his ears.*
> *Afterwards he saw him in private and admonished him:*
> *"Keep thy belief hidden.*
> *He* [God] *knows* [all] *secrets: conceal thy desire."*
> *He* [Bilal] *said: "I repent before thee, O prince."*

There was much repenting of this sort,
[Till] at last he became quit of repenting,
And proclaimed and yielded up his body to tribulation,
Crying: "O Muhammad! O enemy of
  vows and repentance!
O thou with whom my body and all my veins are
  filled!
How should there be room therein for repentance?
Henceforth I will banish repentance from this heart.
How should I repent of the life everlasting?"
Love is the All-subduer, and I am subdued by Love:
By Love's blindness I have been made bright like the sun.

O fierce wind, before Thee I am a straw:
How can I know where I shall fall?
Whether I am Bilal or the new moon,
I am running on and following the course of Thy sun.
What has the moon to do with stoutness or thinness?
She runs at the heels of the sun, like a shadow.
The lovers have fallen into a fierce-torrent:
They have set their hearts on the ordinance of Love.
[They are] like the millstone turning round and round
Day and night and moaning incessantly.[59]

---

59 *Mathnawi*, Book 1, translated by Nicholson.

VII

Human love
for fellow-humans

A believer who loves God is expected to love His people and be kind to them. The Prophet said: "O servant of God, let your love and hate be for the sake of God, because no one can attain to the *wilayah* (guardianship) of God without that, and no one shall find the taste of faith without that, though his prayers and fast be great in number."[60] If one's love and hate are to be only for the sake of God, it would be impossible not to love His people.

On the necessity of love for people, we see that the Qur'an praises those members of the Household of the Prophet who fasted three days and gave everyday the little food that they had at home successively to a poor man, an orphan, and a prisoner: 'And they give food out of love for Him to the poor and the orphan and the captive. [They tell them:]We only feed you for God's sake: we desire from you neither reward nor thanks.' (76: 8 & 9)

There is a well-known *hadith* narrated in different sources that the Prophet said: "People are all God's family, so the dearest people to Him are those who benefit His family the most."[61]

According to a *hadith* and similar to what is mentioned in the New Testament (Mt. 25: 31-46), on the Day of Judgement God will ask some people why they did

---

60 Majlesi, 1983, Vol. 27, p. 54
61 e.g. Hemyari, 1417 A.H., p. 56

not visit Him when He was sick, why they did not feed Him when He was hungry and why they did not give Him water when He was thirsty. Those people will ask: How could these have happened, while you are the Lord of all the world? Then God will reply: So and so was sick and you did not visit him, so and so was hungry and you did not feed him and so and so was thirsty and you did not give water to him. Did not you know that if you did so you would find Me with him?[62]

Thus, in Islam love plays an essential role in ethics, mysticism, theology and even philosophy. To draw an Islamic picture of the world, including the story of the creation of the universe and mankind and then god's treatment of humanity one always needs to invoke the notion of love. God Himself is love and has created the world out of love. He treats human beings with love. Faith also starts with love, an overwhelming love for certain truths, and is required to flourish by the nourishment of this love to the extent that one's love for God fills all of one's heart and directs all aspects of one's life. Love for God can increase only when we reduce our selfishness, and if we can ultimately get rid of selfishness we will be a perfect person whose will and pleasure would be the will and pleasure of God. Love for God and freedom from selfishness can be secured at first by sacrifice and losing our desires for the sake of God and His people and then by having no desire other than what He desires and no will other than His. Then, of course, there will be no sacrifice and no pain. Ethical rules are guidelines to this path of love, enlightened and oriented by teachings of the intellect and the prophets.

---

62 For example, see al-Hilli, 1982, p. 374

Conclusion

Both Christianity and Islam hold love to be the central notion of their faith. In Christianity, love is the greatest virtue (1 Cor. 13: 13) and the commandment of love is the first and the greatest commandment (Mark 12: 28-31, Mt. 22: 34-40, Luke 20: 25-28). In Islam, love is 'the firmest handhold of the faith'[63] and 'the faith is love and love is the faith'[64]

In both religions, love is attributed to God as well as to human beings. However, Divine love is different from human love. Divine love is substantive, a property, since God Himself is love.[65] In the case of humanity, love is a predicate, something accidental to and removable from their essence.

Divine love is eternal. He loves us with an eternal and everlasting love. He created the world and human beings out of love.

God loves mankind so immensely that He has created everything on the earth for their sake. (In Christianity, e.g. Psalms 8: 4-8; In Islam, e.g. the Qur'an 2: 29 & 45: 13)

In Christianity, God's love for man is quite often seen in a parental form. It is also sometimes compared to love of a bridegroom for his bride. In Islam, a more abstract

---

63 e.g. al-Kulayni, 1397 A.H., p. 126

64 Ibid., p. 125

65 In Christianity, e.g. 1 John 4: 8-16; In Islam, it is an established idea among Muslim philosophers and many theologians regarding all Divine attributes: God is love as He is knowledge e.g. al-Shirazi, 1378 A.H., Vol. 2, p. 274

and transcendental attitude towards God and His love is adopted. God's love for man is far greater than that of a mother or a father for his child. God is never addressed as a father or a bridegroom. In Islam, the nearest thing I know of to the parental paradigm, and not that of a bridegroom and bride, is what can be found in some *hadiths*, and not in the Qur'an, that people are considered as His *'yaal*. This term can roughly be translated as family, but its accurate meaning is a group of people that a person takes care of and towards whom he is responsible for their living expenses. In this way, it includes one's parents or even strangers, such as orphans that one has undertaken to pay for. Therefore, God is not presented as father and people are not presented as His children – or even his family. Of course, God loves all people and provides all people and even non-humans with the means of their subsistence.

God's love has an ideal and selfless quality and He does not gain anything from the love itself or from the beloved. God has created the world to 'show forth His own truth and goodness and beauty.'[66] He has created men 'to be known'.[67]

In Christianity and Islam, love for God is universal; it is practised by all creatures. For example, St Augustine says: "O God, Who art loved knowingly or unknowingly by everything capable of loving." Ibne Arabi says: "Nothing other than God has ever been loved."

In both traditions, human love for God extends to fellow humans. Naturally those who are believed to be closer to Him deserve more love. In Christianity, some of the important phrases of the New Testament (1 John 4: 7 - 5: 4)

---

66 Graham, 1939, p. 37

67 e.g. Majlesi, 1983, Vol. 87, p. 344

unveil the need to love one's fellow Christians. Love for neighbour extends to outsiders as well. It even includes enemies. Jesus says: "But I say to you, 'Love your enemies and pray for those who persecute you…' " (Mt. 5: 43 - 45)

In Islam, a most distinguished Qur'anic title of the Prophet Muhammad is 'mercy unto all beings', *rahamatum lil'aalimeen*. During the war of Uhud, when many of his companions, including his uncle Hamzah, were martyred by pagans of his own tribe and he himself was injured and his tooth was broken, the Prophet said: "O my Lord! Please, guide my people. Surely they do not know." So instead of cursing them he prayed for them. The Prophet Muhammad has announced that his mission is 'to complete the noble characteristics.' The list of noble characteristics includes: visiting those who do not visit you, giving and donating to those who do not give or donate to you, and being fair and benevolent towards those who have not been observing your rights. This is something more than just reciprocating people's favours to oneself.

However, the concept of love in Islam is interwoven with that of hatred. Love for God and for the good has to be accompanied by hatred for the devil. In Islam, faith does not become complete unless one's emotions and affections are all directed by devotion to God. A person of faith cannot hate what or whom God loves, just as he cannot love His enemies. God does not love 'any ungrateful sinner' (Qur'an 9: 108), 'the unjust' (Qur'an 3: 57 & 11: 40), 'who is proud, boastful' (Qur'an 4: 36) and 'who is treacherous' (Qur'an 4: 107).

In this way, Islam distinguishes between loving a person and loving his acts or character. You may love a person and still hate his deeds or character. Sometimes your love for him requires you to help him and advise him and sometimes requires you to stop him and, if necessary, fight him. This is the only thing that a truly loving and compassionate parent or friend can do in respect of a criminal and murderer.

Thus, in principle there seems to be no disagreement between Christianity and Islam on the concept of love, though historically Christians and Muslims might have emphasised different aspects or might have practised it differently. Similar facts can also be found among different schools of the same religion.

Bibliography

Augustine, St. (1962) *The Confessions*, edited by E.B. Pusey, (London: Dent)

Barrosse, T. (1967) 'Love (in the Bible)' in *New Catholic Encyclopedia*, Vol. 8, prepared by an editorial staff at the Catholic U. (New York: McGrawHill), pp. 1043, 1044

Bernard, St. (1937), *On the Love of God*, (London: Burns Oates andWashbourne)

Brett, P. (1992), *Love Your Neighbour*, (London: Darton, Longman and Todd)

Cerini, M. (1992), *God Who Is Love*, (New York: New City Press)

Chervin, R. (1973), *Church of Love*, (Los Angeles California: Liguori)

Chittick, W. C. (1987), *The Psalms of Islam*, English translation from *Al-Sahifat Al-Kamilat Al-Sajjadiyya* by Imam Zayn al-Abidin Ali ibn al-Husayn, (Great Britain and Northern Ireland: The Muhammadi Trust)

Clément, O. (1993), *The Roots of Christian Mysticism*, (London: New City)

Edwards, D. (1999), 'Religion' in *The New Fontana Dictionary of Modern Thought* edited by Allan Bullock and Stephen Trombley, (Third edition, London: Harper Collins Publishers, First published 1997), p. 745

Fletcher, J. (1966), *Situation Ethics*, (London: SCM Press Ltd.)

Frankena, W. K. (1973), *Ethics*, (Second edition, U.S.A: Prentice Hall, First published 1963)

Gilleman, G.A. (1967) 'Love (in Theology)' in *New Catholic Encyclopedia*, prepared by an editorial staff at the

Catholic U. (New York: McGraw-Hill), pp. 1044, 1045.

Graham, D. A. (1939), *The Love of God*, (London: Longmans, Green and Co. Ltd)

Johann, R.O. (1967) 'Love' in *New Catholic Encyclopedia*, prepared by an editorial staff at the Catholic U. (New York: McGrawHill), pp. 1039-1043.

Johnston, W. (1978), *The Inner Eye of Love: Mysticism and Religion*, (William Collins Sons and Co. Ltd.)

Lewisohn, L. (1995), *Beyond Faith and Infidelity: The Sufi poetry and Teachings of Mahmud Shabistari*, (Surrey: Curzon Press)

MacNamara, V. (1989), *The Truth in Love: Reflections on Christian Morality*, (Ireland: Gill and Macmillan Ltd.)

Markham, I. (1998), '*Religion and Ethics*', Encyclopedia of Applied Ethics, Volume 3 (Academic Press)

Nasr, S. H. (1989), 'God' in *Islamic Spirituality*, Vol. I (London: SCM Press Ltd.), pp. 311-323

Preston, R. (1996), 'Christian Ethics', *A Companion to Ethics*, edited by Peter Singer (Oxford: Blackwell Publishers, First published 1991), pp. 91-105

Razavi, M.A. (1997), *Suhrawardi and the School of Illumination* (Surrey: Curzon Press)

Shomali, M.A. (1996), *Self-Knowledge* (Tehran: International Publishimg Co.)

Siraj ed-Din, A. (1989), '*The Nature and Origin of Sufism*' in *Islamic Spirituality*, Vol. I (London: SCM Press Ltd.), pp. 223-238

Williams, B. (1997), 'Ethics', *Philosophy: A Guide through the Subject*, edited by A.C. Grayling, (Oxford University Press, First published 1995), pp. 545-582

Catechism of the Catholic Church, (1999), Revised edition (London: Geoffrey Chapman)

The Revised Catechism,(1996), Authorised by the General Synod of the Church of England (Great Britain: Hart-Talbot Ltd.)

Arabic & Persian

al-Daylami (1370 A.H.), **Irshad al-Qulub** (Najaf: al-Matba'at al-'ilmeyyah)

al-Hilli, Allamah (1982), N*ahj al-Haqq wa Kashf al-Sidq*(Qum: Razi & Bidar)

al-Kulayni, M.(1397 A.H.), *Usul al-Kafi* (Tehran: Dar al-Kutub al-Islamiyyah)

al-Shirazi, Sadr ud-din (1378 A.H.), *Al-Asfar al-Aqliyah*, (Qum: Mostafavi)

Avecinna (1375 A.H.), *Al-Ishara*t (Qum: al-Nashr al-Balaghah)

Avecinna (1956), *Al-Ilahiyyat al-Shifa* (Cairo: Al-Matba'atul Amireyyah)

Hemyari (1417 A.H.), *Qurb al-Isnad* (Qum: Muassesat al-Thiqafat al-Islameyyah)

Ibn Arabi, M. (1994), *Al-Futuhat al-Makkeyyah* (Beirut: Darul Fikr)

Majlesi M. (1983), *Bihar al-Anwar* (Beirut: al-Wafa)

Modarresi, S. M. R. (1997), *Ethics*, (Tehran: Soroosh Press)